It's a
Narwhal!

by Mari Schuh

BUMBA BOOKS™

LERNER PUBLICATIONS ◆ MINNEAPOLIS

Note to Educators:

Throughout this book, you'll find critical thinking questions. These can be used to engage young readers in thinking critically about the topic and in using the text and photos to do so.

For Cami and Avery —MS

Lerner Publications Company
A division of Lerner Publishing Group, Inc.
241 First Avenue North
Minneapolis, MN 55401 USA

For reading levels and more information, look up this title at www.lernerbooks.com.

Library of Congress Cataloging-in-Publication Data

Names: Schuh, Mari C., 1975– author.
Title: It's a narwhal! / Mari Schuh.
Other titles: It is a narwhal!
Description: Minneapolis : Lerner Publications, [2018] | Series: Bumba books. Polar animals | Audience: Ages 4–7. | Audience: K to grade 3. | Includes bibliographical references and index.
Identifiers: LCCN 2018000241 (print) | LCCN 2017057031 (ebook) | ISBN 9781512482850 (eb pdf) | ISBN 9781512482829 (lb : alk. paper) | ISBN 9781541526945 (pb : alk. paper)
Subjects: LCSH: Narwhal—Juvenile literature. | Animals—Polar regions—Juvenile literature.
Classification: LCC QL737.C433 (print) | LCC QL737.C433 S38 2018 (ebook) | DDC 599.5/43—dc23

LC record available at https://lccn.loc.gov/2018000241

Manufactured in the United States of America
1-43315-33135-4/6/2018

Table of
Contents

Narwhals in the Sea

Narwhals are small whales.

They swim in groups.

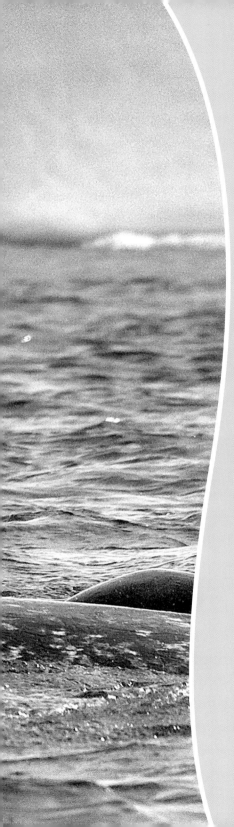

Many narwhals have a tusk.

Some males have two tusks.

Most females do not have a tusk.

The tusk is a long tooth.

It is straight.

Grooves cover the tusk.

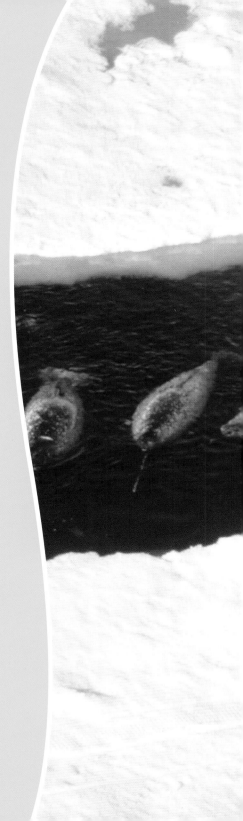

Narwhals swim in the Arctic.

The water there is very cold.

Can you guess what other animals swim in cold water?

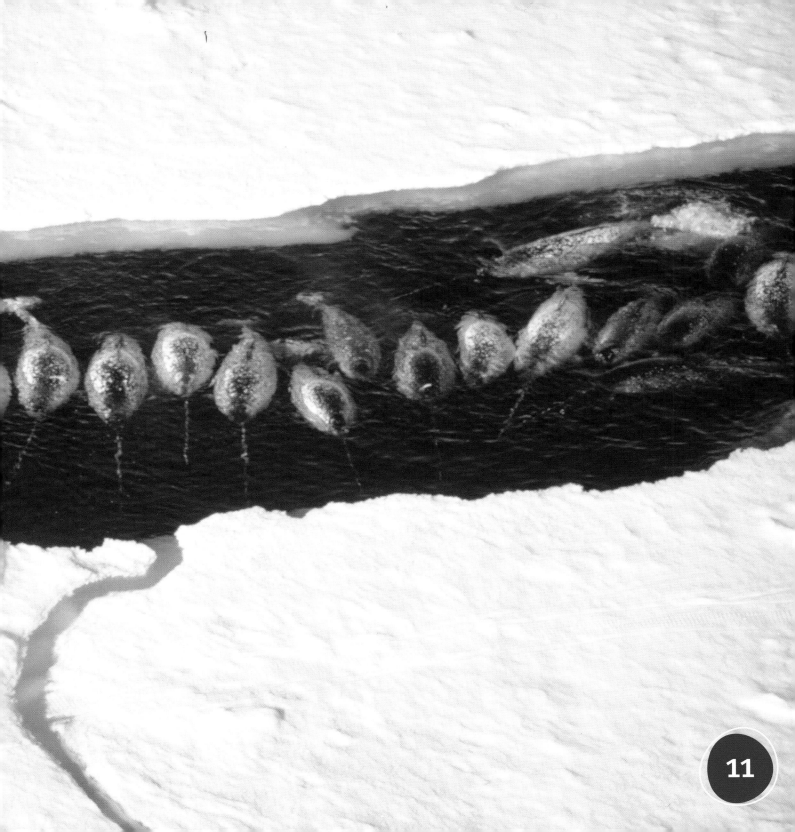

Narwhals swim by the

shore in the summer.

In the winter, they move

out to sea.

A narwhal is slow.

But it can be fast.

It moves quickly to

escape predators.

How might a narwhal's body shape help it swim?

Orcas hunt narwhals.

Polar bears hunt them too.

Narwhals dive deep into

the water.

The water is very dark.

They hunt for food.

Then they come up for air.

Narwhals eat mostly fish.

They eat shrimp and squid too.

They suck up their food.

They swallow it whole!

Parts of a Narwhal

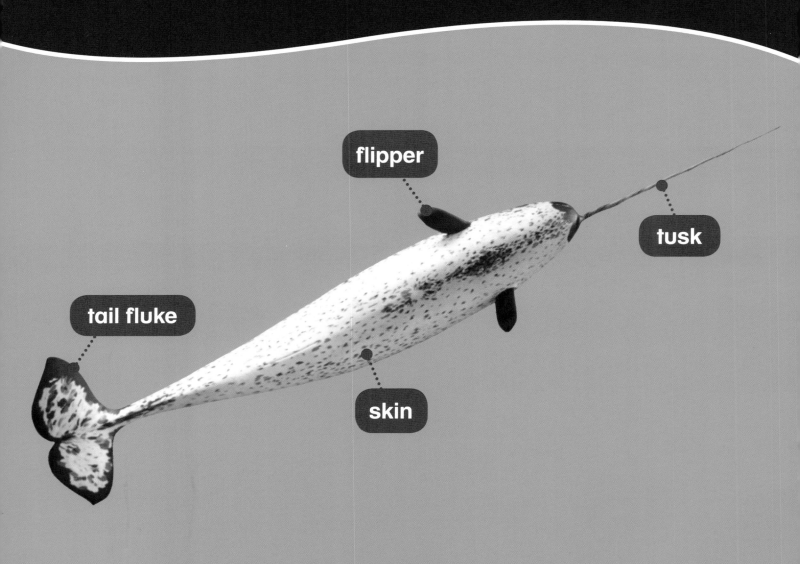

flipper

tusk

tail fluke

skin

Picture Glossary

grooves

long, narrow cuts or marks

predators

animals that hunt and eat other animals

shore

land that is next to a body of water

tusk

a very long, straight tooth that sticks out above a narwhal's mouth

Read More

Boothroyd, Jennifer. *Let's Visit the Ocean.* Minneapolis: Lerner Publications, 2017.

Carr, Aaron. *Narwhal.* New York: AV2 by Weigl, 2016.

Higgins, Nadia. *Oceans.* Minneapolis: Jump!, 2017.

Index

Photo Credits

Image credits: Flip Nicklin/Minden Pictures/Getty Images, pp. 5, 8, 11, 12, 15, 19, 21, 23 (bottom left); Michelle Valberg/All Canada Photos/Getty Images, p. 6; FloridaStock/Shutterstock.com, pp. 16, 23 (top right); Dave Fleetham/Design Pics/Getty Images, p. 22; Science & Society Picture Library/Getty Images, p. 23 (top left); Daryl Bensony/Photographer's Choice/Getty Images, p. 23 (bottom left).

Cover: Dave Fleetham/Design Pics/Getty Images.